Wonderful weekly English practice from CGP!

This book is packed with brilliant Workouts to help Year 2 pupils practise their English skills in 10-Minute chunks every week.

Each Workout covers a mixture of topics — all carefully matched to the Year 2 English curriculum. Use them for starter activities, recaps, homework tasks... or any way that suits you!

We've also included a progress chart and full answers, so it's easy to track how pupils are getting on. It's all worked out beautifully...

Published by CGP
ISBN: 978 1 78908 314 9

Editors: Eleanor Claringbold, Hannah Roscoe, Matt Topping

With thanks to Andy Cashmore and Lucy Towle for the proofreading.

With thanks to Jan Greenway for the copyright research.

Contents pages © Crown Copyright, National Curriculum. Contains public sector information licensed under the Open Government Licence v3.0 - http://www.nationalarchives.gov.uk/doc/open-government-licence/version/3/

Images throughout the book from www.edu-clips.com

Printed by Elanders Ltd, Newcastle upon Tyne.

Based on the classic CGP style created by Richard Parsons.

Text, design, layout and original illustrations
© Coordination Group Publications Ltd. (CGP) 2019
All rights reserved.

Photocopying this book is not permitted, even if you have a CLA licence.
Extra copies are available from CGP with next day delivery • 0800 1712 712 • www.cgpbooks.co.uk

How to Use this Book

- This book contains 36 workouts. We've split them into 3 sections, one for each term, with 12 workouts each. There's roughly one workout for every week of the school year.

- Each workout is out of 15 marks and should take about 10 minutes to complete.

- Each workout tests a variety of English content from the government's programme of study, including grammar, punctuation, spelling, comprehension and writing skills.

- The first 3 workouts only contain Year 1 English content — they're ideal for reminding pupils what they learnt in the previous year. These workouts should be done at the start of Year 2.

- The last 9 workouts only contain Year 2 content — they're perfect for preparing pupils for the Key Stage 1 English SATS tests.

- The other workouts contain a mix of old and new topics.

- As the book progresses, the tests increase in difficulty. If pupils are struggling with the terminology, they can turn to the glossary on p.85.

- Answers can be found at the back of the book.

The contents page will help you identify which Year 2 statutory requirement is being tested in each workout. You can use these to pick the workout which best suits you and the needs of your class (but remember the later in the book, the harder the workout will be, so it's best to save the workouts towards the end of the book for later in the year).

There is a tick box next to each workout on the contents page. Use this to record which tests have been attempted. You can also use the progress chart to track pupils' scores.

Contents — Autumn Term

- Workout 1 2
  - Recap of Year 1 material
- Workout 2 4
  - Recap of Year 1 material
- Workout 3 6
  - Recap of Year 1 material
- Workout 4 8
  - The 'j' sound spelt 'ge' and 'dge'
  - Full stops and capital letters
- Workout 5 10
  - The 's' sound spelt 'c'
  - The suffixes 'er' and 'est'
- Workout 6 12
  - The 'n' sound spelt 'kn' and 'gn'
  - The past tense
- Workout 7 14
  - The 'r' sound spelt 'wr'
  - Apostrophes for singular possession
- Workout 8 16
  - The 'l' sound spelt 'le'
  - The use of commas in lists
- Workout 9 18
  - The 'l' sound spelt 'el'
  - Question marks and exclamation marks
- Workout 10 20
  - The 'l' sound spelt 'al'
  - Co-ordinating conjunctions
- Workout 11 22
  - Words ending in 'il'
  - Types of sentence (statement, question, command, exclamation)
- Workout 12 24
  - The suffix '-ness'
  - The long 'i' sound spelt 'y'

Contents — Autumn Term

- [x] **Workout 1** 2
  - Recap of Year 1 material

- [x] **Workout 2** 4
  - Recap of Year 1 material

- [x] **Workout 3** 6
  - Recap of Year 1 material

- [x] **Workout 4** 8
  - The 'j' sound spelt 'ge' and 'dge'
  - Full stops and capital letters

- [x] **Workout 5** 10
  - The 's' sound spelt 'c'
  - The suffixes 'er' and 'est'

- [x] **Workout 6** 12
  - The 'n' sound spelt 'kn' and 'gn'
  - The past tense

- [x] **Workout 7** 14
  - The 'r' sound spelt 'wr'
  - Apostrophes for singular possession

- [x] **Workout 8** 16
  - The 'l' sound spelt 'le'
  - The use of commas in lists

- [x] **Workout 9** 18
  - The 'l' sound spelt 'el'
  - Question marks and exclamation marks

- [x] **Workout 10** 20
  - The 'l' sound spelt 'al'
  - Co-ordinating conjunctions

- [x] **Workout 11** 22
  - Words ending in 'il'
  - Types of sentence (statement, question, command, exclamation)

- [x] **Workout 12** 24
  - The suffix '-ness'
  - The long 'i' sound spelt 'y'

Contents — Spring Term

☑ **Workout 1** 26
  • Adding '-es' to nouns and verbs ending '-y'
  • Noun phrases

☑ **Workout 2** 28
  • Adding the suffixes '-ed' and '-ing' to words ending '-y' with a consonant before it
  • Co-ordinating conjunctions

☑ **Workout 3** 30
  • Adding the suffix '-ing' to words ending '-e' with a consonant before it
  • Forming compound words

☑ **Workout 4** 32
  • Adding the suffixes '-ed' and '-ing' to words of one syllable ending in a single consonant after a single vowel
  • The suffixes '-ful' and '-less'

☑ **Workout 5** 34
  • The 'or' sound spelt 'a' before 'l' and 'll'
  • The present progressive

☑ **Workout 6** 36
  • The short 'u' sound spelt 'o'
  • Apostrophes for contractions

☑ **Workout 7** 38
  • The long 'e' sound spelt 'ey'
  • The past progressive

☑ **Workout 8** 40
  • Using the suffix '-ly' to turn adjectives into adverbs
  • The short 'o' sound spelt 'a' after 'w' and 'qu'

☑ **Workout 9** 42
  • The 'er' sound spelt 'or' after 'w'
  • Apostrophes for singular possession

☑ **Workout 10** 44
  • The 'or' sound spelt 'ar' after 'w'
  • Subordinating conjunctions

☑ **Workout 11** 46
  • The 'zh' sound spelt 's'
  • The suffixes '-er' and '-est'

☑ **Workout 12** 48
  • The suffixes '-ment' and '-ness'
  • Subordinating conjunctions

Contents — Summer Term

☑ **Workout 1** 50
  • Words ending in '-tion'
  • Apostrophes for contractions

☑ **Workout 2** 52
  • Homophones and near-homophones
  • Capital letters, full stops, question marks and exclamation marks

☑ **Workout 3** 54
  • Common exception words
  • Forming compound words

☑ **Workout 4** 56
  • Recap of Year 2 material

☑ **Workout 5** 58
  • Recap of Year 2 material

☑ **Workout 6** 60
  • Recap of Year 2 material

☑ **Workout 7** 62
  • Recap of Year 2 material

☑ **Workout 8** 64
  • Recap of Year 2 material

☑ **Workout 9** 66
  • Recap of Year 2 material

☑ **Workout 10** 68
  • Recap of Year 2 material

☑ **Workout 11** 70
  • Recap of Year 2 material

☑ **Workout 12** 72
  • Recap of Year 2 material

Progress Chart 74

Answers 75

Glossary 85

Autumn Term: Workout 1

Warm up

1. Circle the **correct spelling** of each word in **bold**.

   I turned the computer **of** / **off**.

   Dan has a **black** / **blacc** cat.

   2 marks

2. Write the **correct spelling** of the word in **bold** on the line.

   I went to buy a **drinck**. ....

   1 mark

3. Add '**s**' or '**es**' to the words below to make them **plural**.

   glass.......... star.......... chair..........

   3 marks

4. Add in **full stops** to the text below.

   Sati likes playing sports She plays rugby every Monday Rugby is her favourite sport.

   2 marks

5. Circle the **three nouns** in the text below.

   Becky saw the bear in the forest.

   3 marks

6. Read the passage and answer the questions.

   > Robbie was getting tired as he climbed up the slope. He knew it was dangerous, but Robbie was a brave explorer. Finally, he reached the top. He was just about to take a photo when he felt the ground rumble beneath his feet.

   What is Robbie's job?

   ....

   Write '**true**' or '**false**' for each sentence.

   Robbie's climb is very easy.   ....

   Robbie gets to the top.   ....

   Circle one word which could replace the word '**rumble**'.

   dance   shake   explode   rise

   4 marks

   Score:

Autumn Term: Workout 2

Warm up

1. Circle the **verbs** in the sentence below.

   The cow smiled as she jumped over the moon.

   2 marks

2. Circle the letters you can add to the word '**tie**' to make it mean the **opposite**.

   de   re   un   mis

   1 mark

3. Circle the **correct spelling** of the words in **bold**.

   I **livv** / **live** in a small town.

   We **love** / **lov** to go swimming.

   2 marks

4. Add the **suffixes** '**er**' and '**est**' to each of these **adjectives**.

	'er'	'est'
grand		
long		
hard		

   3 marks

5. Circle the **three** letters that should be **capital letters**.

spain is very hot in the summer.

i am going to colin's house next week.

3 marks

6. Rewrite this passage without the **four** errors.

> Every Saturday, we go to the lake to watch the boates. The lake is nicest than the park because there's a bench to sit on Last week, my friend's boat sanck.

....

....

....

....

....

4 marks

Score:

Autumn Term: Workout 3

Warm up

1. Add the **suffixes** '**ing**' and '**ed**' to each of these verbs.

	'ing'	'ed'
help		
play		

   2 marks

2. Circle the **two** days of the week which are **spelt wrong** and write the correct spellings on the lines.

   Wensday   Friday   Thursday   Saterday

   ....

   2 marks

3. Circle the **correct spelling** of the words in **bold**.

   The **elefant / elephant** had a bath in the river.

   Ellie needed a new **wheel / weel** for her bike.

   Viraj wants to swim with **dolphins / dolfins**.

   3 marks

4. Circle the **adjectives** in this sentence.

   Hugh bought a shiny new car.

   2 marks

5. Add the word '**and**' in the correct place in each sentence.

Leah wants a cat .... her sister .... wants a rabbit.

We can .... go swimming .... we can play a game.

John likes rowing .... he likes .... fishing.

3 marks

6. Read the passage and answer the questions.

> The Vikings lived a long time ago. They were experts at building boats, and they won lots of battles. Most Vikings lived in wooden houses with a fire in the middle of them.

Write **one** thing the Vikings were good at.

....

What were Viking houses made out of?

....

Which word means the same as '**middle**'? Tick one box.

☐ outside   ☐ centre   ☐ edge   ☐ top

3 marks

Score:

Autumn Term: Workout 4

Warm up

1. Circle the **correct spelling** in each pair of words.

    lunch / luntch   cach / catch

    2 marks

2. Write either '**ge**' or '**dge**' to make two words below.

    chan............   bri............

    2 marks

3. Add '**s**' or '**es**' to the words in **bold** to complete the sentences.

    Ed **climb**............ mountains every weekend.

    Adam **teach**............ dancing at the school.

    2 marks

4. Split these words into **syllables**.

    pencil   ....

    sandwich   ....

    tomato   ....

    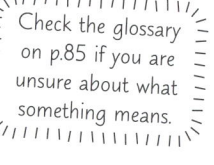

    3 marks

5. Add in **full stops** and circle where **capital letters** should be in the passage below.

annabel played football for the school team she practised football every day

2 marks

6. Rewrite this passage without the **four** errors.

> We slowly walked towards the ege of the jungle. The trees were so tall we couldn't see the top We had come here to see the monkeys. On a high brantch, we saw a monkey swinging through the trees. it was amazing!

....

....

....

....

....

....

4 marks

Score:

Autumn Term: Workout 5

Warm up

1. Add in **full stops** to the passage below.

   Lily wants to win the competition First prize is a trip to London She has to draw the best picture

   3 marks

2. Circle the **correct spelling** of each word.

   fansy   fancee   fancy   fanci

   isy   icy   icey   icee

   2 marks

3. Add '**er**' or '**est**' correctly to the **adjectives** below.

   Those are the **small**............... shoes I have ever seen.

   My hair is **short**............... than yours.

   A leopard is **fast**............... than a snail.

   3 marks

4. Circle the **correct spelling** of the words in **bold**.

   Jakub enjoyed **paynting** / **painting**.

   The **theef** / **thief** was never seen again.

   2 marks

5. Circle the **adjectives** in these sentences.

   Freya is wearing a yellow coat.

   The trumpet is a loud instrument.

   2 marks

6. Read the passage and answer the questions.

   > Buster was a lazy dragon. He was supposed to guard the treasure, but he loved to have naps. One Sunday, he heard a noise and saw a little boy running away with a gold cup. Buster thought about pursuing him, but instead he let out a big yawn and closed his eyes.

   What was Buster meant to be guarding?

   ....

   Find and copy a word from the text that means the same as '**chasing**'.

   ....

   Why does Buster let the boy go?

   ....

   ....

   3 marks

   Score:

Autumn Term: Workout 6

Warm up

1. Circle the **nouns** in the sentence below.

   The friendly dinosaur lives in a dark cave.

   2 marks

2. Write the **correct spelling** of the word in **bold** on the line.

   James hurt his **nee** while dancing. ....

   The **knome** lived under a tree. ....

   The **gnight** went on an adventure. ....

   3 marks

3. Tick the sentence that is likely to end with an **exclamation mark**.

   Charlotte had salad for lunch ☐

   Watch out for the crocodile ☐

   I like reading adventure books ☐

   1 mark

4. Circle the **correct spelling** in each pair of words.

   stashun / station   fiction / ficsion

   2 marks

5. Rewrite these verbs in the **past tense**.

   talk ....

   test ....

   kick ....

   3 marks

6. Rewrite this passage to make it more **interesting**.

   > Rachel stepped onto the boat. It set off towards the sea. It was windy. Rachel could see the island ahead.

   Rachel stepped onto the small brown boat.

   Use exciting words to make your description come to life. Try to make your sentences different lengths.

   ....

   ....

   ....

   ....

   4 marks

   Score:

Autumn Term: Workout 7

Warm up

1. Make the two sentences below into one sentence using the **joining word** '**and**'.

   Kyle likes drama. He reads books.

   ....

   2 marks

2. Add a '**y**' to the words below to turn them into **adjectives**.

   hair..........   luck..........   cloud..........

   3 marks

3. Add a missing **silent letter** to each of the words below.

   ....rong   ....riter   ....reck

   3 marks

4. Circle the **two verbs** in the sentence below.

   The frog hopped into the pond and swam away.

   2 marks

5. Add **apostrophes** to the words in **bold** below.

That is **Lucys** coat.

I am going to **Jacks** house.

2 marks

6. Read the passage and answer the questions.

> Billie Jean King is a tennis champion. In 1973, she played a famous match against Bobby Riggs. Bobby believed that women couldn't play tennis as well as men could, and Billie was determined to prove him wrong. She comfortably beat him in the match.

What sport did Billie Jean King play?

....

Find and copy a word from the text that shows that Billie Jean King **really wanted** to win the match.

....

Who won the match?

☐ Bobby Riggs   ☐ Billie Jean King

3 marks

Score:

Autumn Term: Workout 8

Warm up

1. Add **one letter** to the words in **bold** so they are spelt correctly.

    The **clif**.......... was very high.

    Bumblebees **buz**..........

    2 marks

2. Circle the **correct spelling** of the words in **bold**.

    My **littal / little** brother is annoying.

    Don't put your shoes on the **table / tabel**.

    2 marks

3. Rewrite the sentence below with the correct **capital letters**.

    we will be at diana's party in april.

    ....

    3 marks

4. Write the **correct spelling** of the word in **bold** on the line.

    Animah had lost a **glov**.   ....

    Can you **proov** you're right?   ....

    2 marks

5. Add **one comma** to each list below.

   My mum grows carrots onions and potatoes.

   For Christmas, I'd like books sweets and a dog.

   2 marks

6. Rewrite this passage without the **four** errors.

   > On safari, we saw lions giraffes and zebras. Jamals favourite animal was the giraffe. Sadly, ella missed it because she wasn't feeling very wel.

   4 marks

   Score:

Autumn Term: Workout 9

Warm up

1. Choose a **verb** from the box to complete each sentence.

   | kick   ride |

   I know how to .... a bike.

   In football, you have to .... the ball.

   2 marks

2. Circle the **correct spelling** in each pair of words.

   modle / model   panel / panal

   2 marks

3. Write the **correct spelling** of the word in **bold** on the line.

   The pirate had to walk the **planc**. ....

   1 mark

4. Circle the **correct spelling** of the words in **bold**.

   The **dinosore / dinosaur** was hungry.

   Steven does gymnastics every **night / nite**.

   We need to **shair / share** the cake.

   3 marks

5. Add a **question mark** or an **exclamation mark** in the boxes below.

    Do you like ice cream ☐

    Look at the spider ☐

    How do you get to the bus stop ☐

    3 marks

6. Rewrite this passage so it is all in the **past tense**. There are **four** verbs you'll need to change.

    > I am in the park with two of my best friends. As we walk down the path, a big brown dog jumps in front of us. I stop to stroke its soft fur.

    ....

    ....

    ....

    ....

    4 marks

    Score: ☐

Autumn Term: Workout 10

Warm up

1. Add '**s**' or '**es**' to each of these words to make them **plural**.

    pencil............   class............   window............

    3 marks

2. Circle the **correct spelling** of the words in **bold**.

    We need to go to the **hospital** / **hospitle**.

    My favourite **animel** / **animal** is a sloth.

    This is the **finel** / **final** time I'll ask you to do it.

    3 marks

3. Tick the sentences which need a **question mark**.

    What did you do at the weekend ☐

    Andrew likes to play hockey ☐

    Can you see the moon tonight ☐

    2 marks

4. Circle the word that is **spelt wrong** in the sentence below. Write the correct spelling on the line.

    It is going to be sunny on Tusday.

    ....

    2 marks

5. Complete the sentence below with a **joining word**.

He was going to the zoo, ... the car broke down.

1 mark

6. Read the poem and answer the questions.

> **Bella the Magic Cat**
>
> You will only see her,
> In the dark of night.
> Everybody tells me,
> She's a peculiar sight.
>
> I have never seen her,
> But I think it's true.
> She casts spells with her tail,
> Then disappears from view.

When does Bella the Magic Cat come out?

....

Which word best describes Bella the Magic Cat?

☐ scary   ☐ strange   ☐ happy   ☐ angry

How does Bella the Magic Cat do magic?

....

4 marks

Score:

Autumn Term: Workout 11

Warm up

1. Choose an **adjective** from the box to complete the sentences below.

   | smart   quick |

   The journey was very ....

   Nathan had .... shoes.

   2 marks

2. Add '**s**' or '**es**' to the verbs in **bold**.

   The camel **walk**........... in the desert.

   Tanmay **go**........... to the park every weekend.

   2 marks

3. Circle the **correct spelling** in each pair of words.

   pupul / pupil   nostril / nostral

   2 marks

4. Add **two letters** to the word '**happy**' so the sentence means the **opposite**.

   Orla was very ....**happy**.

   1 mark

5. Draw lines to match each sentence to the **correct label**.

What a surprise! — command

What do you want for dinner? — exclamation

Open the book to page 3. — statement

Giraffes have purple tongues. — question

4 marks

6. Rewrite this passage to make it more **interesting**.

> Drew looked out of the window. The rocket landed on the surface of the Moon. The Earth looked different from space.

Use exciting words to make your description come to life. Try to make your sentences different lengths.

Drew was excited as he peered out of the window. ....

....

....

....

....

4 marks

Score:

Autumn Term: Workout 12

Warm up

1. Add '**ness**' to the words below to turn them into **nouns**.

   kind............   weak............   thick............

   3 marks

2. Circle the **two adjectives** in this sentence.

   The little fish had beautiful scales.

   2 marks

3. Circle the **correct spelling** in each pair of words.

   dry / drie   fleye / fly

   2 marks

4. Split these words into **syllables**.

   penguin   ....

   banana   ....

   computer   ....

3 marks

5. Rewrite the passage below with **full stops**.

   The dog is excited to go for a walk I don't want to take it

   ....

   ....

   2 marks

6. Read the passage and answer the questions.

   > Niamh needed to get away from the noise of the city. She walked and walked until she reached the forest. It was quiet. Leaves from the trees rustled gently, and Niamh stopped a while to catch her breath. That was better.

   How does Niamh get to the forest?

   ....

   Why do you think Niamh goes to the forest?

   ....

   ....

   Tick the best word to describe what the forest is like.

   ☐ noisy   ☐ busy   ☐ peaceful   ☐ spooky

   3 marks

   Score: ☐

Spring Term: Workout 1

Warm up

1. Tick the box next to a **full sentence**.

    Varun loves to cook. ☐

    without going to the bank ☐

    1 mark

2. Make the words below **plural**.

    fly ....   lady ....

    ruby ....   baby ....

    4 marks

3. Tick the phrase that is a **noun phrase**.

    the slimy monster ☐

    get dressed ☐

    1 mark

4. Circle the word that is spelt **wrong** in the sentence below. Write the correct spelling on the line.

    My dog loves to fech the ball on the beach.

    ....

    2 marks

5. Draw lines between the words that can join together to make **compound words**.

bath		boy
sun		set
cow		tub

3 marks

6. Rewrite this passage without the **four** errors.

> Mrs Torrance keeps her ponys on a pach of grass by the river. Yesterday, i went to feed them with her, but one pony looked evul, so I ran away.

....

....

....

....

....

4 marks

Score:

Spring Term: Workout 2

Warm up

1. Add the **suffixes** '**ing**', '**ed**' and '**er**' to the verb '**paint**' to make three new words.

   paint............   paint............   paint............

   2 marks

2. Rewrite the words below in the **correct order** to form a sentence.

   reading   liked   Alex   magazines

   ....

   1 mark

3. Circle the **correct spelling** of the words in **bold**.

   Frosty was made out of **snoe / snow**.

   We are going to Iceland next **year / yeer**.

   Lucy has long **hair / hare**.

   3 marks

4. Write the **correct spelling** of the words in **bold**.

   I **studyed** history.   ....

   She is **carrieing** a book.   ....

   2 marks

5. Add '**and**', '**or**', or '**but**' to the sentences below.

We can either go to a café .... we can eat at home.

Olivia went to Egypt .... she saw a crocodile.

Ben was going to read, ... he forgot his book.

3 marks

6. Rewrite this passage in the **present tense**.
There are **four verbs** you'll need to change.

> The witch chopped up some nettles and berries for her potion. Then, she sprinkled in some fairy dust and stirred the mixture. To finish, she poured the potion into six little bottles.

....

....

....

....

....

....

....

4 marks

Score:

Spring Term: Workout 3

Warm up

1. Add the **suffixes** '**ing**' and '**ed**' to each of these **verbs**.

	'ing'	'ed'
cook		
sort		

   2 marks

2. Add a **missing letter** to each word in **bold**.

   I lost a **soc**.......... in the changing room.

   Tom played **jaz**.......... music at his party.

   2 marks

3. Circle the **correct spelling** in each pair of words.

   bakeing / baking   smiling / smileing

   2 marks

4. Use the words in the box to make **compound words** to complete the sentences.

cut	fish	hair	paste	gold	tooth

   We have a pet .... called Frank.

   You've got .... on your chin!

   Joel needs a ....

   3 marks

5. Add **full stops** to the text below.

Anna has been learning to play the violin for five years She wants to be the best violinist in Scotland On Tuesdays, she plays in a band

3 marks

6. Rewrite each set of sentences using '**and**', '**or**' or '**but**' to **join** the sentences together.

The diver put on his suit. He jumped into the water.

……………………………………………………

……………………………………………………

He wanted to find some turtles. The sea was too rough.

……………………………………………………

……………………………………………………

He might try again later. He might go to a lake instead.

……………………………………………………

……………………………………………………

3 marks

Score:

Spring Term: Workout 4

Warm up

1. Add a **full stop** or a **question mark** in the boxes below.

    Do you know what time the train arrives ☐

    Peter wants to visit the zoo ☐

    2 marks

2. Circle the **correct spelling** of the words in **bold**.

    Anaya is **huming / humming** a tune.

    Kris **patted / pated** the dog.

    2 marks

3. Write the **correct spelling** of the words in **bold**.

    Snakes shed their **scin**. ....

    Pam did a **scetch** of a tree. ....

    2 marks

4. Add the **suffixes** 'ful' and 'less' to these **nouns** to turn them into **adjectives**.

	'ful'	'less'
colour		
thought		
hope		

    3 marks

Spring Term: Workout 4

5. Circle the nouns which should have a **capital letter**.

sofa   october   vase   mirror

ireland   oscar   hippo   sunday

2 marks

6. Read the passage and answer the questions.

> Yellowstone is a beautiful National Park in North America. Many types of wildlife live there, such as grizzly bears, mountain goats and wolves. Lots of people go to visit the park's impressive waterfalls and forests.

Where is Yellowstone National Park?

....

Write down **two** animals you might see in Yellowstone.

....

....

What do you think '**impressive**' might mean?

☐ ugly   ☐ small   ☐ amazing   ☐ boring

4 marks

Score:

Spring Term: Workout 4

Spring Term: Workout 5

Warm up

1. Choose a **noun** from the box to complete the sentences below.

   | aeroplane   Canada   suitcase |

   We are going to .... on holiday.

   We will get on an ....

   I need to pack a ....

   3 marks

2. Circle the **correct spelling** of the words in **bold**.

   There are dolphins in the **see / sea**.

   The **night / knight** climbed the tall tower.

   2 marks

3. Add the **suffixes** 'ing', 'ed' or 'er' to the words in **bold** below.

   Megan **help**............ her dad wash the car.

   The **teach**............ told the class to sit down.

   Luke is **draw**............ a picture of me.

   3 marks

4. Circle the **correct spelling** in each pair of words.

talk / taulk   allways / always

2 marks

5. Circle the correct word to complete the sentence below.

| ran | | runs | | running |

Rami is .... away from the tiger.

1 mark

6. Rewrite this passage using the **joining words** '**and**', '**or**' or '**but**' to **link** sentences together.

> David loved being outside. He was quite tired. Joy threw a pebble into the pond. She saw the water ripple. They could stay there. They could go back to their tent instead.

....

....

....

....

....

4 marks

Score:

Spring Term: Workout 6

Warm up

1. Circle the word that is **spelt wrong** in the sentence below. Write the correct spelling on the line.

   I don't know what the cloo means.

   ....

   2 marks

2. Circle the **correct spelling** of the words in **bold**.

   Jenny fights with her **brother** / **bruther**.

   Nuthing / **Nothing** is better than chocolate.

   I don't like **Mondays** / **Mundays**.

   3 marks

3. Add an **apostrophe** in the **correct place** to the words below.

   cant   theyre   isnt

   3 marks

4. Add the **missing letter** to the word in **bold**.

   Mark **thi**..........**ks** comic books are great.

   1 mark

5. Rewrite the sentence below with the correct **capital letters**.

in july, i'm going to japan with him.

....

2 marks

6. Read the passage and answer the questions.

> Amelia's big moment had finally arrived — her first ever wheelchair race. She looked around nervously. A small crowd had gathered to watch. Amelia gripped the edges of her wheels and focused her eyes on the end of the track. "Ready, set, go!"

How many wheelchair races has Amelia done before?

....

How does Amelia feel before the race starts?

....

Find and copy a word from the text that means '**held**'.

....

What happens in the last sentence of the story?

....

4 marks

Score:

Spring Term: Workout 7

Warm up

1. Add a **prefix** to the words below to make them mean the **opposite**.

   Check the glossary on p.85 if you're not sure what something means.

   ....tidy   ....fair

   2 marks

2. Tick the sentences which use **full stops** and **question marks** correctly.

   What is your favourite colour. ☐

   There are five cupcakes left. ☐

   I can see the statue. from my house ☐

   Can you pass me a napkin? ☐

   2 marks

3. Circle the **correct spelling** in each pair of words.

   key / kee   honey / honny

   vallee / valley donkie / donkey

   4 marks

4. Circle the **compound word** in each sentence.

   The postman walked up the path.

   I saw a dragonfly near the river.

   2 marks

5. Circle the correct word to complete the sentence below.

   | mowing | mowed | mow |

   Linda was .... the lawn.

   1 mark

6. Rewrite this passage using **noun phrases** to make it more **interesting** and **descriptive**.

   The squirrel sniffed the ground. It started digging through the leaves. It was looking for an acorn.

   You can add other words to nouns to describe them. These noun phrases will make your description come to life.

   ....

   ....

   ....

   ....

   ....

   4 marks

   Score:

Spring Term: Workout 8

Warm up

1. Write the words in the correct order to form a **sentence**.

   | maths | Laura | her | does | homework |

   ....

   1 mark

2. Add '**ly**' to the words below to turn them into **adverbs**.

   slow.......... neat.......... quiet..........

   3 marks

3. Circle the **correct spelling** of the words in **bold**.

   There's a **wosp / wasp** in the classroom!

   We **wont / want** some orange juice.

   Dad is hanging out the **washing / woshing**.

   3 marks

4. Circle the words that need **capital letters**.

   nobody else was at the park on monday. ben and I played on the swings. we stayed there until teatime.

   2 marks

5. Write either '**ph**' or '**wh**' to complete the words below.

tele..........one ....isker gra..........

3 marks

6. Rewrite this passage in the **past tense**.
   There are **six verbs** you'll need to change.

   > I climb into the hot-air balloon. I untie the ropes and the balloon floats upwards. Everything below me looks tiny. The view is incredible! I watch the sky carefully.

   ....

   ....

   ....

   ....

   ....

   ....

   ....

3 marks

Score:

Spring Term: Workout 9

Warm up

1. Circle the **correct spelling** of the words in **bold**.

   I fell over and made my trousers **dirty / dirtee**.

   How **sunnie / sunny** it is today!

   2 marks

2. Circle the **correct spelling** in each pair of words.

   wurk / work   worth / werth

   2 marks

3. Add **suffixes** to the words below to make them **plural**.

   scooter............   gas............

   wish............   ribbon............

   2 marks

4. Add '**er**' or '**est**' to the **adjectives** in the sentences below.

   This path to the pet shop is the **quick**............ .

   I am much **kind**............ than my friends.

   You always laugh the **loud**............ in class.

   3 marks

5. Circle the **two** words that should have an **apostrophe**.

   Zaynas parents came to watch the play.

   The crocodiles tail was long and scaly.

   2 marks

6. Read the passage and answer the questions.

   > Giant redwoods are some of the tallest trees on Earth. They can grow to a colossal 90 m in height. That's almost as tall as Big Ben! Their bark is reddish-brown in colour and it's also very thick. This helps to shield the trees from wildfires.

   What do you think '**colossal**' might mean?

   ☐ medium ☐ surprising ☐ tiny ☐ huge

   Which building is only just taller than giant redwoods?

   ....

   Why do you think these trees are called 'redwoods'?

   ....

   Find and copy a word from the text that means '**protect**'.

   ....

   4 marks

   Score: ☐

Spring Term: Workout 10

Warm up

1. Rewrite the sentence in the correct order with **capital letters** in the correct places.

    larry the coat nibbled sheep the

    ....

    2 marks

2. Circle the **correct spelling** in each pair of words.

    war / wor   dworf / dwarf   warmth / wormth

    3 marks

3. Tick the pair of sentences which could be **joined together** using the word '**and**'.

    We can visit Jane. We can stay here instead. ☐

    She fell over. She grazed her elbow. ☐

    1 mark

4. Circle the word that is **spelt wrong**. Write the correct spelling on the line.

    mowth   about   mouse

    ....

    2 marks

5. Underline the **joining words** in the sentences below.

My dog gets scared when it thunders.

They are angry because they lost the game.

She will get into trouble if she's late.

I already knew that it was true.

4 marks

6. Read the passage and answer the questions.

> Ali stared at the tin box. It had a small silver padlock holding it shut. He shook the box and he felt its contents gently slide back and forth. It made hardly any noise at all. Ali was desperate to open the box, so he looked around the room for the key.

How can you tell that the contents of the box are soft?

....

Write the numbers 1 to 4 in the boxes below to show the **order of events** in the passage.

Ali shakes the box. ☐   Ali looks for the key. ☐

Ali notices the padlock. ☐   Ali looks at the box. ☐

3 marks

Score:

Spring Term: Workout 11

Warm up

1. Choose a **verb** from the box to complete each sentence.

   run   hide   runs   hides

   She .... in the cupboard.

   They .... home after school.

   2 marks

2. Circle the **correct spelling** of each word.

   uzual / usual   televijion / television

   2 marks

3. Add '**y**' correctly to each of the words below.

   smile   chat   sponge

   ....

   3 marks

4. Complete the words below with the correct **letters**.

   Curtis is cooking dinner in the **ki**............**en**.

   Treena **stre**............**ed** her arms above her head.

   2 marks

5. Circle the word where the **suffix** has been added **correctly** to the word in **bold**.

   dirty   dirtier   dirter   dirtyer

   heavy   heavyest   heavest   heaviest

   2 marks

6. Rewrite this passage using the **joining words** '**but**', '**when**' or '**because**' to replace the full stops in **bold**. Only use each joining word **once**.

   > Rita's favourite season was summer**.** She also loved winter. She always wore her yellow scarf**.** It was snowing outside. Inside her cabin, it was very cosy**.** She had a log fire.

   ....

   ....

   ....

   ....

   ....

   ....

   4 marks

   Score:

Spring Term: Workout 12

Warm up

1. Add either '**ment**' or '**ness**' to make two new words below.

   mad.................... enjoy....................

   2 marks

2. Circle the **correct spelling** of the words in **bold**.

   Paul **said / sed** my singing was beautiful.

   We visit our cousins **wonse / once** a month.

   2 marks

3. Circle the word that is **spelt wrong** in the sentence below. Write the correct spelling on the line.

   I dressed up as a sceleton.

   ....

   2 marks

4. Complete the sentences by putting a **full stop**, an **exclamation mark** or a **question mark** in each box.

   What a long walk this is ☐   I'm quite tired ☐

   Are we near the lake yet ☐   I'd like to sit down ☐

   2 marks

5. Circle the correct **joining word** to complete each sentence.

Come to my house **that / if** you want to play.

She had to stay at home **because / that** she was ill.

This is the film **when / that** I saw last week.

We will start **that / when** everyone has arrived.

4 marks

6. Rewrite this passage without the **six** errors.

> The children scipped excitedlie across the playground? The teacher appeared at the gate with a box ov toys. He place it on the floor and took out the skipping ropez.

....

....

....

....

....

3 marks

Score:

Summer Term: Workout 1

Warm up

1. Tick the sentence that is likely to end with an **exclamation mark**.

    Don't let the cows escape ☐

    Please can you feed the hamster ☐

    1 mark

2. Add the **missing pair of letters** to each word in **bold**.

    I **pre**..........**ed** the button and waited for the lift.

    The wolf had a **flu**..........**y** grey coat.

    2 marks

3. Circle the word that is **spelt wrong**. Write the correct spelling on the line.

    direction   creasion   section

    ....

    2 marks

4. Rearrange each set of letters to make **three adjectives** ending in 'er' or 'est'.

    a r w e r m   d e a r r k   s l c o e d t

    ....

    3 marks

5. Circle the **correct version** of the **bold** words in each sentence.

   I **didn't / did'nt** break the vase.

   Kyle thinks that **yo'ure / you're** mean.

   She'd / Sh'ed rather stay at home.

   3 marks

6. Rewrite this passage to make it more **interesting**.

   > The artist put the paint onto the paper. She mixed the colours. She spread the paint everywhere. It looked good!

   The artist squirted the paint onto .... the blank paper. ....

   Use exciting words to make your description come to life. Try to make your sentences different lengths.

   ....

   ....

   ....

   ....

   ....

   4 marks

   Score: [ ]

Summer Term: Workout 2

Warm up

1. Add a **prefix** to the word '**wrap**' so the sentence means the **opposite**.

   Kelly was excited to ....**wrap** her present.

   1 mark

2. Circle the word that is **spelt wrong** in the sentence below. Write the correct spelling on the line.

   There was a rainbbow above the playground.

   ....

   2 marks

3. Circle the **correct spelling** of the words in **bold**.

   Leopards can't change **their / there** spots.

   A **bee / be** landed on Joe's flowers.

   2 marks

4. Circle the **four adjectives** in the sentences below.

   Erin's favourite plants are very colourful.
   She's put them in cute round pots.

   2 marks

5. Add a **question mark**, an **exclamation mark** or a **full stop** in the boxes below. Circle the one letter that should be a **capital letter**.

I really hate eating broccoli ☐ My sister enjoys it with nearly every meal ☐ do you like broccoli, Ibrahim ☐

4 marks

6. Rewrite this passage using **commas** to separate the words in each list. You'll need to add **four** commas.

> Alexa likes to play rugby cricket tennis and football. Lydia Lisa and Anja play cricket with her. Their next match will be on Monday Friday or Sunday.

....

....

....

....

....

4 marks

Score: ☐

Summer Term: Workout 3

Warm up

1. Circle the **two nouns** in the sentence below.

   The snake flicked its tongue and hissed.

   1 mark

2. Circle the **correct spelling** in each pair of words.

   clim / climb   path / parth

   door / dore   only / ownly

   4 marks

3. Write either '**ph**' or '**wh**' to make **two words** below.

   I went on a trip to take ....**otographs**
   of blue ....**ales**.

   2 marks

4. Circle the **question marks**, **exclamation marks** and **full stops** that are in the **wrong place**. There are **four** you'll need to circle.

   It was nearly the end. of the holiday. Elana was sad! to be leaving. What a great time? they'd had! Where will they go! next year?

   2 marks

5. Add a **noun** to each word to make **compound words**.

black + ... = ...

tooth + ... = ...

light + ... = ...

3 marks

6. Rewrite this passage using the **joining words** 'and', '**but**' or '**because**' to replace the full stops in **bold**.

> My brother gets up early on Sundays**.** He delivers newspapers. He does it to earn pocket money**.** He really enjoys it. Usually he gets home at 10 am**.** Sometimes he gets home later.

Only use each joining word once.

....

....

....

....

....

....

3 marks

Score:

Summer Term: Workout 4

Warm up

1. Make the adjectives into **adverbs** by adding the suffix '**ly**'.

   sweet .... hungry ....

   2 marks

2. Circle the **correct spelling** in each pair of words.

   chardge / charge   gester / jester

   gem / jem   hedge / hege

   2 marks

3. Write the **plural** of each word on the lines below.

   relay .... copy ....

   reply .... turkey ....

   4 marks

4. Write the **correct spelling** of the word in **bold** on the line.

   This is your final **wawning**.   ....

   Ross moved **towords** the door.   ....

   2 marks

5. Add **commas** to the lists in the sentences below.

On his way to school, Tobias passes the library the park the vet's and the bank.
He usually sees cars motorbikes buses and Mr Bolt on his tractor.

2 marks

6. Read the passage and answer the questions.

> Giant squids are mysterious sea creatures which live in very deep water. This means that people hardly ever see them in the wild. They can grow longer than a double-decker bus, and adults can weigh the same as a giant panda. Their eyes are as large as dinner plates.

Which word means the same as '**hardly ever**'?

☐ always   ☐ sometimes   ☐ never   ☐ rarely

What animal can giant squids weigh the same as?

....

Are their eyes bigger or smaller than human eyes?

....

3 marks

Summer Term: Workout 5

Warm up

1. Circle the **correct spelling** in each pair of words.

    easier / easyer   cosyist / cosiest

    2 marks

2. Circle the word that is **spelt wrong** in the sentence below. Write the correct spelling on the line.

    I have been to lots of big sities.

    ....

    2 marks

3. Tick the **two commands**.

    Put on a coat before going out. ☐

    I put the eggs in the fridge. ☐

    Stir the mixture slowly. ☐

    2 marks

4. Circle the **correct verb** to complete each sentence.

    I am **walk / walking** through the woods.

    The sun is **shining / shines** brightly.

    The birds **is / are** singing in the trees.

    3 marks

5. Underline the **noun phrases** in the sentences below.

   I have a large white rabbit.

   The brown cow sniffed the fresh green grass.

   3 marks

6. Rewrite this passage in the **present tense**. There are **six verbs** you'll need to change.

   > Everybody loved Ned the unicorn. He was the greatest superhero ever! His long cape flapped as he glided through the air. If anyone ever needed help, Ned came to the rescue.

   ....

   ....

   ....

   ....

   ....

   ....

   3 marks

   Score:

Summer Term: Workout 6

Warm up

1. Add a **noun** to the word below to make a **compound word**.

   snow + ... = ...

   1 mark

2. Rearrange the letters below to make **three words** beginning with '**kn**' or '**gn**'.

   o k t n   w g a n   f e n k i

   ....

   3 marks

3. Write the **correct spelling** of the word in **bold** on the line.

   The pirate stole the **shiney** treasure.   ....

   Carl was a deep-sea **divr**.   ....

   2 marks

4. Choose a **suffix** to complete each of the words below.

   | er   ness   ment |

   rude............   play............   base............

   3 marks

5. Complete the sentences below with 'if' or 'when'.

   I want to be a doctor .... I grow up.

   I will go to the party .... you come too.

   2 marks

6. Read the passage and answer the questions.

   > Deserts are areas of dry land with very little water. The world's largest desert is the Sahara in North Africa.
   >
   > Deserts can be very hot, so many animals hide underground during the day. At night, they come out to search for food.

   Where is the Sahara desert?

   ....

   Put a tick in each row to show whether each statement is **true** or **false**.

	true	false
Deserts are dry places.		
Deserts are always cold.		

   Why do you think many desert animals search for food at night?

   ....

   4 marks

   Score:

Summer Term: Workout 7

Warm up

1. Circle the **correct spelling** in each pair of words.

   torking / talking   netball / netbawl

   2 marks

2. Circle the word that is **spelt wrong** in the sentence below. Write the correct spelling on the line.

   Jamie has broken his rist.

   ....

   2 marks

3. Circle the **correct spelling** of the words in **bold**.

   The ice cream was very **runy / runny**.

   Chetna bought a new food **mixer / mixxer**.

   2 marks

4. Add the **suffixes** '**ful**' or '**less**' to these **nouns** to turn them into **adjectives**.

   penny   ....

   plenty   ....

   2 marks

5. Underline the words that should have an **apostrophe**.

Shauns class went to a farm. The farms owner was called David. He had a herd of cows. All of Davids family worked on the farm.

3 marks

6. Rewrite this passage to make it more **interesting**.

> The door made a noise as Sam pushed it open. He shone the torch into the room. Everything was dusty. There were spiders everywhere.

The old door creaked loudly as Sam gently nudged it open.

Use exciting words to make your description come to life. Try to make your sentences different lengths.

4 marks

Score:

Summer Term: Workout 8

Warm up

1. Tick the sentence that uses **tenses correctly**.

   I waved to her when I see her. ☐

   He tidied the house before they arrived. ☐

   1 mark

2. Circle the **correct spelling** in each pair of words.

   saddle / saddel   turtul / turtle   ankle / ankul

   3 marks

3. Add a **question mark**, an **exclamation mark** or a **full stop** in the boxes below. Underline the one word that should have a **capital letter**.

   I was looking for my shoes, but I couldn't find them ☐
   Where could they be ☐ "if I don't find them
   soon, I'll be late for the bus ☐ " I shouted.

   4 marks

4. Circle the **correct spelling** of the words in **bold**.

   Tom had to **measure / meazure** the line.

   It was an important **decizion / decision**.

   2 marks

5. Add a **suffix** to the words in **bold** to complete each sentence.

   Mum thanked me for being **help**............. .

   Amir was **care**............. and dropped the vase.

   2 marks

6. Rewrite this passage using the **joining words** '**or**', '**but**' or '**when**' to replace the full stops in **bold**.

   > Nial wanted to buy some roses for Polly. The shop didn't have any left**.** He could buy daffodils. He could buy tulips instead. Nial always bought Polly flowers**.** It was her birthday.

   ....

   ....

   ....

   ....

   ....

   ....

   3 marks

   Score: [ ]

Summer Term: Workout 9

Warm up

1. Label each sentence as a **statement** or a **command**.

   Don't eat any sweets. ....

   I will eat some sweets. ....

   2 marks

2. Circle the word that is **spelt wrong** in the sentence below. Write the correct spelling on the line.

   The train raced into the tunnle.

   ....

   2 marks

3. Add '**ing**' to the **most sensible verb** to complete the sentence.

   | drink | eat | listen |

   The horse is .... the carrots.

   1 mark

4. Write the correct **punctuation** in the boxes.

   How thirsty I am ☐ I need to drink something ☐

   Could I have some water please ☐

   3 marks

Summer Term: Workout 9

5. Rewrite the words in **bold** in the **present tense**.

Rita **watched** .... the surfer ride the wave.

He **drifted** .... across the water, then

he **fell** .... off his surfboard.

3 marks

6. Read the passage and answer the questions.

> As I swam deeper into the icy lake, the sunlight faded away. I knew I would have to come up for air soon. Just as I was about to turn back, I saw a faint light peeking through a gigantic group of fish. I swam towards it, eager to discover what it was. As I got closer, I realised that it was an underwater palace...

Which **two** adjectives best describe the lake?

☐ bright   ☐ dark   ☐ boiling   ☐ cold

Why does the narrator nearly turn back?

....

What was the faint light coming from?

....

4 marks

Score:

Summer Term: Workout 10

Warm up

1. Circle the **correct spelling** in each pair of words.

   squoshed / squashed   squad / squod

   2 marks

2. Write the **correct spelling** of the word in **bold** on the line.

   Liam gave the **signul** to run.   ....

   I always have **cerele** for breakfast.   ....

   2 marks

3. Circle the word that is **spelt wrong** in the sentence below. Write the correct spelling on the line.

   The angry monkey stole the monie.

   ....

   2 marks

4. Add **commas** to the text below.

   My dad gave me a sandwich some crisps and an apple for my lunch. The sandwich had cheese ham lettuce and tomato in it.

   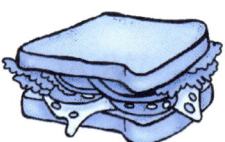

   3 marks

5. Circle the word where the **suffix** has been added **correctly** to the word in **bold**.

day	dayly	dayily	daily
shy	shylly	shyly	shyily

2 marks

6. Rewrite this passage to make it more **interesting**. Use **noun phrases** to make it more descriptive.

> The man stood on the beach. He watched the sea ripple. There were lots of fish in the water. The man took out his camera.

You can add other words to nouns to describe them. These noun phrases will make your description come to life.

....

....

....

....

....

....

4 marks

Score:

Summer Term: Workout 11

Warm up

1. Circle the **correct spelling** in each pair of words.

    cement / sement   rice / risce

    2 marks

2. Write the **correct spelling** of the word in **bold** on the line.

    Luke gave me a green **pencell**. ....

    I am on the school **counsul**. ....

    2 marks

3. Tick the pair of sentences which could be **joined together** using '**but**'.

    The lions roared. They were angry. ☐

    Olga called me. I didn't hear the phone. ☐

    1 mark

4. Complete the sentences below with '**was**' or '**were**'.

    Malika .... lying on the sofa.

    She wanted to have a nap, but her cats .... making lots of noise.

    2 marks

5. Shorten these words using an **apostrophe**.

   I am ....   they have ....

   it is ....   she will ....

   4 marks

6. Rewrite this passage in the **past tense**.
   There are **eight verbs** you'll need to change.

   > The eagle soars across the sky and calls to her chicks. She has some food for them. She lands in the nest and gives the chicks a fish. They eat it eagerly. The eagle flaps her wings and smiles.

   ....

   ....

   ....

   ....

   ....

   ....

   ....

   4 marks

   Score:

Summer Term: Workout 12

Warm up

1. The words below are **spelt wrong**.
   Write the **correct spelling** of each word on the line.

   cuvver   shuve   anuther

   ....

   3 marks

2. Circle the **correct spelling** of the words in **bold**.

   Jade refused to **replie / reply** to her teacher.

   This year, I will **try / treye** to be more kind.

   2 marks

3. Circle the **correct spelling** of each word.

   werm   wurm   worm   wirm

   wirld   world   wurld   worled

   2 marks

4. Underline all the **joining words** in the text below.

   Harry was happy that Martha had forgiven him.
   He never meant to upset her. He had hidden
   Martha's teddy bear, but he gave it back to her.

   2 marks

5. Rewrite the sentence below in the **past tense**.

   I speak to her before I go home.

   ....

   2 marks

6. Read the passage and answer the questions.

   > The knight walked nervously through the maze. If he found the diamond, the queen would reward him. If he stole any gold, she would punish him. After a while, the knight turned a corner and saw a pile of gold coins. He thought about what the queen had said, and about how rich the gold would make him...

   How can you tell that the knight is scared?

   ....

   What does the queen want the knight to find?

   ....

   Do you think the knight will steal the gold?

   Tick one box: Yes ☐   No ☐

   Why do you think this?

   ....

   4 marks

   Score:

Progress Chart

Fill in the progress chart after you finish each workout.

Put your scores in here to see how you've done. Each workout is out of 15 marks.

	Autumn Term	Spring Term	Summer Term
Workout 1			
Workout 2			
Workout 3			
Workout 4			
Workout 5			
Workout 6			
Workout 7			
Workout 8			
Workout 9			
Workout 10			
Workout 11			
Workout 12			

Answers

Autumn Term

Workout 1 — pages 2-3

1. off   1 mark
   black   1 mark
2. drink   1 mark
3. glass**es**   1 mark
   star**s**   1 mark
   chair**s**   1 mark
4. Sati likes playing sports. She plays rugby every Monday. Rugby is her favourite sport.   1 mark for each correct answer
5. Becky   bear   forest
   1 mark for each correct answer
6. explorer   1 mark
   false   1 mark
   true   1 mark
   shake   1 mark

Workout 2 — pages 4-5

1. smiled   jumped
   1 mark for each correct answer
2. un   1 mark
3. live   1 mark
   love   1 mark
4.

	'er'	'est'
grand	grander	grandest
long	longer	longest
hard	harder	hardest

   1 mark for each pair of words spelt correctly
5. **S**pain is very hot in the summer.
   I am going to **C**olin's house next week.
   1 mark for each correct answer
6. Every Saturday, we go to the lake to watch the **boats**. The lake is **nicer** than the park because there's a bench to sit on**.** Last week, my friend's boat **sank**.
   1 mark for each error correctly rewritten

Workout 3 — pages 6-7

1.

	'ing'	'ed'
help	helping	helped
play	playing	played

   1 mark for each pair of words spelt correctly
2. Wednesday   1 mark for circling 'Wensday' and rewriting it correctly
   Saturday   1 mark for circling 'Saterday' and rewriting it correctly
3. elephant   1 mark
   wheel   1 mark
   dolphins   1 mark
4. shiny   new
   1 mark for each correct answer
5. Leah wants a cat **and** her sister wants a rabbit.
   We can go swimming **and** we can play a game.
   John likes rowing **and** he likes fishing.
   1 mark for each correct answer
6. E.g. building boats   1 mark
   wood   1 mark
   centre   1 mark

Workout 4 — pages 8-9

1. lunch   1 mark
   catch   1 mark
2. chan**ge**   1 mark
   bri**dge**   1 mark

3. Ed climb**s** mountains every weekend.   1 mark
    Adam teach**es** dancing at the school.   1 mark

4. pen cil   1 mark
    sand wich   1 mark
    to ma to   1 mark

5. (A)nnabel played football for the school team. (S)he practised football every day.
    2 marks for all 4 correct, otherwise 1 mark for any 2 correct

6. We slowly walked towards the **edge** of the jungle. The trees were so tall we couldn't see the top. We had come here to see the monkeys. On a high **branch**, we saw a monkey swinging through the trees. **I**t was amazing!
    1 mark for each error correctly rewritten

Workout 5 — pages 10-11

1. Lily wants to win the competition. First prize is a trip to London. She has to draw the best picture.
    1 mark for each correctly placed full stop

2. fancy   1 mark
    icy   1 mark

3. Those are the **smallest** shoes I have ever seen.   1 mark
    My hair is **shorter** than yours.   1 mark
    A leopard is **faster** than a snail.   1 mark

4. painting   1 mark
    thief   1 mark

5. yellow   1 mark
    loud   1 mark

6. treasure   1 mark
    pursuing   1 mark
    E.g. Because Buster is too lazy to chase him.
    1 mark

Workout 6 — pages 12-13

1. dinosaur   cave
    1 mark for each correct answer

2. knee   1 mark
    gnome   1 mark
    knight   1 mark

3. Watch out for the crocodile   1 mark

4. station   1 mark
    fiction   1 mark

5. talked   1 mark
    tested   1 mark
    kicked   1 mark

6. Any sensible answer.
    Award 1-2 marks for answers that have only made minor changes to the original passage, e.g. adjectives or adverbs added.
    Award 3-4 marks for answers that have changed the passage more significantly, e.g. more developed descriptions or have attempted to vary the sentence lengths.

Workout 7 — pages 14-15

1. Kyle likes drama **and** he reads books.
    1 mark for 'and' in the correct place, and 1 mark for the sentence being correctly punctuated.

2. hairy   1 mark
    lucky   1 mark
    cloudy   1 mark

3. wrong   1 mark
    writer   1 mark
    wreck   1 mark

4. hopped   swam
    1 mark for each correct answer

5. That is Lucy's coat.   1 mark
    I am going to Jack's house.   1 mark

6. tennis   1 mark
    determined   1 mark
    Billie Jean King   1 mark

Answers

© CGP — not to be photocopied

Workout 8 — pages 16-17

1. cli**ff** 1 mark
   bu**zz** 1 mark

2. litt**le** 1 mark
   tab**le** 1 mark

3. **W**e will be at **D**iana's party in **A**pril.
   1 mark for each correct answer

4. **g**love 1 mark
   prove 1 mark

5. My mum grows carrots**,** onions and potatoes.
   1 mark
   For Christmas, I'd like books**,** sweets and a dog.
   1 mark

6. On safari, we saw lions**,** giraffes and zebras. Jamal's favourite animal was the giraffe. Sadly, **Ella** missed it because she wasn't feeling very **well**.
   1 mark for each correct answer

Workout 9 — pages 18-19

1. I know how to **ride** a bike. 1 mark
   In football, you have to **kick** the ball.
   1 mark

2. mo**del** 1 mark
   pa**nel** 1 mark

3. pla**nk** 1 mark

4. di**n**osaur 1 mark
   night 1 mark
   s**h**are 1 mark

5. Do you like ice cream**?** 1 mark
   Look at the spider**!** 1 mark
   How do you get to the bus stop**?** 1 mark

6. I **was** in the park with two of my best friends. As we **walked** down the path, a big brown dog **jumped** in front of us. I **stopped** to stroke its soft fur. 1 mark for each word correctly rewritten in the past tense

Workout 10 — pages 20-21

1. pencil**s** 1 mark
   class**es** 1 mark
   window**s** 1 mark

2. hospital 1 mark
   animal 1 mark
   final 1 mark

3. What did you do at the weekend? 1 mark
   Can you see the moon tonight? 1 mark

4. Tuesday 1 mark for circling 'Tusday', and 1 mark for rewriting it correctly

5. E.g. but 1 mark

6. E.g. at night 1 mark
   strange 1 mark
   E.g. she casts spells with her tail 2 marks

Workout 11 — pages 22-23

1. quick 1 mark
   smart 1 mark

2. walk**s** 1 mark
   go**es** 1 mark

3. pupil 1 mark
   nostril 1 mark

4. Orla was very **un**happy. 1 mark

5. What a surprise! — exclamation
   What do you want for dinner? — question
   Open the book to page 3. — command
   Giraffes have purple tongues. — statement
   1 mark for each correct answer

6. Any sensible answer.
   Award 1-2 marks for answers that have only made minor changes to the original passage, e.g. adjectives or adverbs added.
   Award 3-4 marks for answers that have changed the passage more significantly, e.g. more developed descriptions or have attempted to vary the sentence lengths.

Workout 12 — pages 24-25

1. kind**ness** 1 mark
   weak**ness** 1 mark
   thick**ness** 1 mark

2. little   beautiful
   1 mark for each correct answer

3. dry 1 mark
   fly 1 mark

4. pen guin 1 mark
   ba na na 1 mark
   com pu ter 1 mark

5. The dog is excited to go for a walk**.** I don't want to take it**.**
   1 mark for each correctly placed full stop

6. she walked 1 mark
   E.g. Because she needed a break from the city 1 mark
   peaceful 1 mark

Spring Term

Workout 1 — pages 26-27

1. Varun loves to cook**.** 1 mark

2. flies 1 mark
   rubies 1 mark
   ladies 1 mark
   babies 1 mark

3. the slimy monster 1 mark

4. fetch 1 mark for circling 'fech', and 1 mark for rewriting it correctly

5. bath — tub 1 mark
   sun — set 1 mark
   cow — boy 1 mark

6. Mrs Torrance keeps her **ponies** on a **patch** of grass by the river. Yesterday, **I** went to feed them with her, but one pony looked **evil**, so I ran away.
   1 mark for each error correctly rewritten

Workout 2 — pages 28-29

1. paint**ing**   paint**ed**   paint**er**
   2 marks for all 3 correct, otherwise 1 mark for any 2 correct

2. Alex liked reading magazines. 1 mark

3. snow 1 mark
   year 1 mark
   hair 1 mark

4. studied 1 mark
   carrying 1 mark

5. We can either go to a café **or** we can eat at home. 1 mark
   Olivia went to Egypt **and** she saw a crocodile. 1 mark
   Ben was going to read, **but** he forgot his book. 1 mark

6. The witch **chops** up some nettles and berries for her potion. Then, she **sprinkles** in some fairy dust and **stirs** the mixture. To finish, she **pours** the potion into six little bottles.
   1 mark for each verb correctly rewritten in the present tense

Workout 3 — pages 30-31

1.

	'ing'	'ed'
cook	cooking	cooked
sort	sorting	sorted

1 mark for each pair of words spelt correctly

2. I lost a soc**k** in the changing room. 1 mark
   Tom played ja**zz** music at his party. 1 mark

3. baking 1 mark
   smiling 1 mark

4. We have a pet **goldfish** called Frank. 1 mark
   You've got **toothpaste** on your chin! 1 mark
   Joel needs a **haircut**. 1 mark

Answers

5. Anna has been learning to play the violin for five years**.** She wants to be the best violinist in Scotland**.** On Tuesdays, she plays in a band**.**
   1 mark for each correctly placed full stop

6. The diver put on his suit **and** he jumped into the water.   1 mark
   He wanted to find some turtles, **but** the sea was too rough.   1 mark
   He might try again later **or** he might go to a lake instead.   1 mark

Workout 4 — pages 32-33

1. Do you know what time the train arrives**?**
   1 mark
   Peter wants to visit the zoo**.**   1 mark

2. humming   1 mark
   patted   1 mark

3. skin   1 mark
   sketch   1 mark

4.
	'ful'	'less'
colour	colourful	colourless
thought	thoughtful	thoughtless
hope	hopeful	hopeless

   1 mark for each pair of words spelt correctly

5. october   ireland   oscar   sunday.
   2 marks for all 4 correct, otherwise 1 mark for any 2 correct

6. North America   1 mark
   E.g. grizzly bears and mountain goats
   1 mark for each correct answer
   amazing   1 mark

Workout 5 — pages 34-35

1. We are going to **Canada** on holiday.
   1 mark
   We will get on an **aeroplane**.   1 mark
   I need to pack a **suitcase**.   1 mark

2. sea   1 mark
   knight   1 mark

3. Megan help**ed** her dad wash the car.   1 mark
   The teach**er** told the class to sit down.
   1 mark
   Luke is draw**ing** a picture of me.   1 mark

4. talk   1 mark
   always   1 mark

5. running   1 mark

6. E.g. David loved being outside, **but** he was quite tired. Joy threw a pebble into the pond **and** she saw the water ripple. They could stay there, **or** they could go back to their tent instead.
   Award 1-2 marks for answers that have made limited attempts to link sentences effectively.
   Award 3-4 marks for answers that have successfully added joining words in the relevant places, whilst still maintaining separate sentences.

Workout 6 — pages 36-37

1. clue   1 mark for circling 'cloo', and 1 mark for rewriting it correctly

2. brother   1 mark
   Nothing   1 mark
   Mondays   1 mark

3. can't   1 mark
   they're   1 mark
   isn't   1 mark

4. Mark thi**n**ks comic books are great.   1 mark

5. **I**n **J**uly, **I**'m going to **J**apan with him.
   2 marks for all 4 correct, otherwise 1 mark for any 2 correct

6. none   1 mark
   nervous   1 mark
   gripped   1 mark
   E.g. the race begins   1 mark

Workout 7 — pages 38-39

1. **un**tidy   1 mark
   unfair   1 mark

2. There are five cupcakes left.   1 mark
   Can you pass me a napkin?   1 mark

3. key   1 mark
   valley   1 mark
   honey   1 mark
   donkey   1 mark

4. postman   1 mark
   dragonfly   1 mark

5. mowing   1 mark

6. Any sensible answer. Award 1-2 marks for answers that have only made minor changes to the original passage, e.g. one or two words added. Award 3-4 marks for answers that have used more frequent and/or developed noun phrases.

Workout 8 — pages 40-41

1. E.g. Laura does her maths homework.
   1 mark

2. slow**ly**   1 mark
   neat**ly**   1 mark
   quiet**ly**   1 mark

3. wasp   1 mark
   want   1 mark
   washing   1 mark

4. (nobody) else was at the park on (monday). (ben) and I played on the swings. (we) stayed there until teatime.
   2 marks for all 4 correct, otherwise 1 mark for any 2 correct

5. tele**ph**one   1 mark
   whisker   1 mark
   gra**ph**   1 mark

6. I **climbed** into the hot-air balloon. I **untied** the ropes and the balloon **floated** upwards. Everything below me **looked** tiny. The view **was** incredible! I **watched** the sky carefully.
   3 marks for all 6 words correctly rewritten in the past tense, otherwise 1 mark for every 2 words correctly rewritten

Workout 9 — pages 42-43

1. dirty   1 mark
   sunny   1 mark

2. work   1 mark
   worth   1 mark

3. scooter**s**   gas**es**
   wish**es**   ribbon**s**
   2 marks for all 4 correct, otherwise 1 mark for any 2 correct

4. quick**est**   1 mark
   kind**er**   1 mark
   loud**est**   1 mark

5. Zaynas   1 mark
   crocodiles   1 mark

6. huge   1 mark
   Big Ben   1 mark
   E.g. Their bark is red.   1 mark
   shield   1 mark

Workout 10 — pages 44-45

1. Larry the sheep nibbled the coat.
   1 mark for rewriting the words in the correct order, 1 mark for using a capital letter in the correct place

2. war   1 mark
   dwarf   1 mark
   warmth   1 mark

3. She fell over. She grazed her elbow.   1 mark

4. mowth   1 mark for circling 'mowth' and 1 mark for rewriting it correctly

5. when   1 mark
   because   1 mark
   if   1 mark
   that   1 mark

6. E.g. They don't make any noise.   1 mark
Ali shakes the box. — 3
Ali notices the padlock. — 2
Ali looks for the key. — 4
Ali looks at the box. — 1
2 marks for all 4 correct, otherwise
1 mark for any 2 correct

Workout 11 — pages 46-47

1. hides   1 mark
   run   1 mark

2. usual   1 mark
   television   1 mark

3. smiley   1 mark
   chatty   1 mark
   spongy   1 mark

4. ki**tch**en   1 mark
   stre**tch**ed   1 mark

5. dirtier   1 mark
   heaviest   1 mark

6. Rita's favourite season was summer, **but** she also loved winter. She always wore her yellow scarf **when** it was snowing outside. Inside her cabin, it was very cosy **because** she had a log fire.
   Award 1-3 marks for answers that replace the full stops with the correct linking words. Award a further mark for correctly rewriting the passage.

Workout 12 — pages 48-49

1. mad**ness**   1 mark
   enjoy**ment**   1 mark

2. said   1 mark
   once   1 mark

3. skeleton   1 mark for circling 'sceleton', and 1 mark for rewriting it correctly

4. What a long walk this is**!** I'm quite tired**.** Are we near the lake yet**?** I'd like to sit down**.**
   2 marks for all 4 correct, otherwise
   1 mark for any 2 correct

5. Come to my house **if** you want to play.
   1 mark
   She had to stay at home **because** she was ill.
   1 mark
   This is the film **that** I saw last week.   1 mark
   We will start **when** everyone has arrived.
   1 mark

6. The children **skipped excitedly** across the playground**.** The teacher appeared at the gate with a box **of** toys. He **placed** it on the floor and took out the skipping **ropes**.
   3 marks for all 6 errors correctly rewritten, otherwise 1 mark for every 2 errors correctly rewritten

Summer Term

Workout 1 — pages 50-51

1. Don't let the cows escape   1 mark

2. I pre**ss**ed the button and waited for the lift.
   1 mark
   The wolf had a flu**ff**y grey coat.   1 mark

3. creation   1 mark for circling 'creasion', and 1 mark for rewriting it correctly

4. warmer   1 mark
   darker   1 mark
   coldest   1 mark

5. didn't   1 mark
   you're   1 mark
   She'd   1 mark

6. Any sensible answer. Award 1-2 marks for answers that have only made minor changes to the original passage, e.g. adjectives changed or adverbs added. Award 3-4 marks for answers that have changed the passage more significantly, e.g. more developed descriptions added or have attempted to vary the sentence lengths.

Workout 2 — pages 52-53

1. Kelly was excited to **un**wrap her present.
   1 mark

2. rainbow   1 mark for circling 'rainbbow', and 1 mark for rewriting it correctly

3. their   1 mark
   bee   1 mark

4. Erin's (favourite) plants are very (colourful). She's put them in (cute) (round) pots.
   2 marks for all 4 correct, otherwise 1 mark for any 2 correct

5. I really hate eating broccoli! My sister enjoys it with nearly every meal. (Do) you like broccoli, Ibrahim**?**
   1 mark for each correct answer

6. Alexa likes to play rugby**,** cricket, tennis and football. Lydia**,** Lisa and Anja play cricket with her. Their next match will be on Monday**,** Friday or Sunday.
   1 mark for each correctly placed comma

Workout 3 — pages 54-55

1. The (snake) flicked its (tongue) and hissed.
   1 mark for both correct

2. climb   1 mark
   door   1 mark
   path   1 mark
   only   1 mark

3. I went on a trip to take **ph**otographs of blue **wh**ales.   1 mark for each correct answer

4. It was nearly the end(.) of the holiday. Elana was sad(.) to be leaving. What a great time(?) they'd had! Where will they go(?) next year?
   2 marks for all 4 correct, otherwise 1 mark for any 2 correct

5. E.g. black + bird = blackbird   1 mark
   E.g. tooth + brush = toothbrush   1 mark
   E.g. light + house = lighthouse   1 mark

6. E.g. My brother gets up early on Sundays **because** he delivers newspapers. He does it to earn pocket money **and** he really enjoys it. Usually he gets home at 10 am **but** sometimes he gets home later.
   Award 1-3 marks for answers that replace the full stops with the correct linking words.

Workout 4 — pages 56-57

1. sweetly   1 mark
   hungrily   1 mark

2. charge   jester
   gem   hedge
   2 marks for all 4 correct, otherwise 1 mark for every 2 correct

3. relays   1 mark
   replies   1 mark
   copies   1 mark
   turkeys   1 mark

4. warning   1 mark
   towards   1 mark

5. On his way to school, Tobias passes the library**,** the park**,** the vet's and the bank. He usually sees cars**,** motorbikes, buses and Mr Bolt on his tractor.   2 marks for all 4 correct, otherwise 1 mark for any 2 correct

6. rarely   1 mark
   giant panda   1 mark
   bigger   1 mark

Workout 5 — pages 58-59

1. easier   1 mark
   cosiest   1 mark

2. cities   1 mark for circling 'sities', and 1 mark for rewriting it correctly

3. Put on a coat before going out.   1 mark
   Stir the mixture slowly.   1 mark

4. walking   1 mark
   shining   1 mark
   are   1 mark

Answers

5. I have <u>a large white rabbit</u>.   1 mark
   <u>The brown cow</u> sniffed <u>the fresh green grass</u>.
   1 mark for each correct answer

6. Everybody **loves** Ned the unicorn. He **is** the greatest superhero ever! His long cape **flaps** as he **glides** through the air. If anyone ever **needs** help, Ned **comes** to the rescue.
   3 marks for all 6 words correctly rewritten in the present tense, otherwise 1 mark for every 2 words correctly rewritten

Workout 6 — pages 60-61

1. E.g. snow + man = snowman   1 mark

2. knot   1 mark
   gnaw   1 mark
   knife   1 mark

3. shiny   1 mark
   diver   1 mark

4. rude**ness**   1 mark
   play**er**   1 mark
   base**ment**   1 mark

5. I want to be a doctor **when** I grow up.
   1 mark
   I will go to the party **if** you come too.
   1 mark

6. North Africa   1 mark

	true	false
Deserts are dry places.	✓	
Deserts are always cold.		✓

   1 mark for each correct answer
   E.g. It's too hot during the day.   1 mark

Workout 7 — pages 62-63

1. talking   1 mark
   netball   1 mark

2. wrist   1 mark for circling 'rist', and 1 mark for rewriting it correctly

3. runny   1 mark
   mixer   1 mark

4. penniless   1 mark
   plentiful   1 mark

5. <u>Shauns</u> class went to a farm. The <u>farms</u> owner was called David. He had a herd of cows. All of <u>Davids</u> family worked on the farm.
   1 mark for each correct answer

6. Any sensible answer. Award 1-2 marks for answers that have only made minor changes to the original passage, e.g. adjectives changed or adverbs added. Award 3-4 marks for answers that have changed the passage more significantly, e.g. more developed descriptions added or have attempted to vary the sentence lengths.

Workout 8 — pages 64-65

1. He tidied the house before they arrived.
   1 mark

2. saddle   1 mark
   turtle   1 mark
   ankle   1 mark

3. I was looking for my shoes, but I couldn't find them**.** Where could they be**?** "**i**f I don't find them soon, I'll be late for the bus!" I shouted.
   1 mark for each correct answer

4. measure   1 mark
   decision   1 mark

5. help**ful**   1 mark
   care**less**   1 mark

6. Nial wanted to buy some roses for Polly, **but** the shop didn't have any left. He could buy daffodils **or** he could buy tulips instead. Nial always bought Polly flowers **when** it was her birthday.
   Award 1-3 marks for answers that replace the full stops with the correct linking words.

Workout 9 — pages 66-67

1. command   1 mark
   statement   1 mark

2. tunnel   1 mark for circling 'tunnle', and 1 mark for rewriting it correctly

3. The horse is **eating** the carrots.   1 mark

4. How thirsty I am**!** I need to drink something**.** Could I have some water please**?**
   1 mark for each correct answer

5. Rita **watches** the surfer ride the wave. He **drifts** across the water, then he **falls** off his surfboard.
   1 mark for each correct answer

6. dark   1 mark
   cold   1 mark
   E.g. They need to come up for air.   1 mark
   the underwater palace   1 mark

Workout 10 — pages 68-69

1. squashed   1 mark
   squad   1 mark

2. signal   1 mark
   cereal   1 mark

3. money   1 mark for circling 'monie',
   and 1 mark for rewriting it correctly

4. My dad gave me a sandwich**,** some crisps and an apple for my lunch. The sandwich had cheese**,** ham**,** lettuce and tomato in it.
   1 mark for each comma correctly placed

5. daily   1 mark
   shyly   1 mark

6. Any sensible answer. Award 1-2 marks for answers that have only made minor changes to the original passage, e.g. one or two words added. Award 3-4 marks for answers that have used more frequent and/or developed noun phrases.

Workout 11 — pages 70-71

1. cement   1 mark
   rice   1 mark

2. pencil   1 mark
   council   1 mark

3. Olga called me. I didn't hear the phone.
   1 mark

4. Malika **was** lying on the sofa. She wanted to have a nap, but her cats **were** making lots of noise.
   1 mark for each correct answer

5. I'm   1 mark
   it's   1 mark
   they've   1 mark
   she'll   1 mark

6. The eagle **soared** across the sky and **called** to her chicks. She **had** some food for them. She **landed** in the nest and **gave** the chicks a fish. They **ate** it eagerly. The eagle **flapped** her wings and **smiled**.
   4 marks for all 8 words correctly rewritten in the present tense, otherwise 1 mark for every 2 words correctly rewritten

Workout 12 — pages 72-73

1. cover   1 mark
   shove   1 mark
   another   1 mark

2. reply   1 mark
   try   1 mark

3. worm   1 mark
   world   1 mark

4. Harry was happy <u>that</u> Martha had forgiven him. He never meant to upset her. He had hidden Martha's teddy bear, <u>but</u> he gave it back to her.
   1 mark for each correct answer

5. I **spoke** to her before I **went** home.
   1 mark for each verb correctly rewritten in the past tense

6. E.g. He walked nervously through the maze.
   1 mark
   a diamond   1 mark
   E.g. Yes. The knight will be rich if he steals the gold.   2 marks
   or
   E.g. No. The queen will punish the knight if he steals the gold.   2 marks

Answers